Nathaniel Hawthorne's

The Scarlet Letter

Text by
Michael F. Petrus
(M.Ed., Rutgers University)
Department of English
Bridgewater-Raritan High School
Bridgewater, New Jersey

Illustrations by
Thomas E. Cantillon

 Research & Education Association

MAXnotes™ for
THE SCARLET LETTER

Printed in the United States of America

Library of Congress Catalog Card Number 94-65958

International Standard Book Number 0-87891-950-3

MAXnotes™ is a trademark of
Research & Education Association, Piscataway, New Jersey 08854

What **MAXnotes**™ *Will Do for You*

This book is intended to help you absorb the essential contents and features of Nathaniel Hawthorne's *The Scarlet Letter* and to help you gain a thorough understanding of the work. The book has been designed to do this more quickly and effectively than any other study guide.

For best results, this **MAXnotes** book should be used as a companion to the actual work, not instead of it. The interaction between the two will greatly benefit you.

To help you in your studies, this book presents the most up-to-date interpretations of every section of the actual work, followed by questions and fully explained answers that will enable you to analyze the material critically. The questions also will help you to test your understanding of the work and will prepare you for discussions and exams.

Meaningful illustrations are included to further enhance your understanding and enjoyment of the literary work. The illustrations are designed to place you into the mood and spirit of the work's settings.

The **MAXnotes** also include summaries, character lists, explanations of plot, and chapter-by-chapter analyses. A biography of the author and discussion of the work's historical context will help you put this literary piece into the proper perspective of what is taking place.

The use of this study guide will save you the hours of preparation time that would ordinarily be required to arrive at a complete grasp of this work of literature. You will be well-prepared for classroom discussions, homework, and exams. The guidelines that are included for writing papers and reports on various topics will prepare you for any added work which may be assigned.

The **MAXnotes** will take your grades "to the max."

Dr. Max Fogiel
Program Director

Contents

> **Each section includes List of Characters,
> Summary, Analysis, Study Questions and
> Answers, and Suggested Essay Topics.**

SECTION ONE

Introduction

The Life and Work of Nathaniel Hawthorne

Nathaniel Hawthorne's life seems characterized by continued efforts to make enough money to support himself and his family interspersed with creative bursts of writing. He was born in Salem, Massachusetts on July 4, 1804, the second of three children. His father, Captain Hathorne (the writer added the *w* to his name when he began his writing career), was absent at his birth and died at sea when Nathaniel was four years old.

From the ages of nine to twelve Nathaniel was unable to be active or to go to school due to a foot injury. Since he had little interaction with children his own age, he developed a fondness for reading, especially the classics. In the summer of 1816 his mother moved the family to Maine to live on family property there. Here Nathaniel grew to love the freedom of the wilderness.

During the winters Nathaniel returned to Salem for schooling. From 1821 to 1823 he attended Bowdoin College in Brunswick, Maine where he met three men who later influenced his life. One was Henry Wadsworth Longfellow, the well-known poet. The second, Franklin Pierce, became the fourteenth president of the United States and later was able to help Hawthorne financially with a political appointment. The third, Horatio Bridge, helped Hawthorne publish his first collection of stories.

After graduation Hawthorne spent the next twelve years at his mother's house reading voraciously and practicing his writing skills.

During this time he had only a few short works published. In 1837 his college classmate Bridge helped him publish *Twice-Told Tales*, a collection of stories which brought him some notice as a writer, but not very much income.

When he became engaged to Sophia Peabody in 1839, Hawthorne, needing more income, took a position in the Custom House at Boston. He did not enjoy the job and was not able to write very much during this period. In 1841 he invested a thousand dollars in Brook Farm, an experimental community in Massachusetts where he thought he could support himself with labor and be free to write. Finding himself too exhausted to write, he left after a few months. Encouraged by increased income from magazine writing, Nathaniel and Sophia were married in Boston on July 9, 1842.

The newly married couple moved to Concord, Massachusetts. There, while living in the now-famous "Old Manse," Hawthorne came to know many leading Transcendentalist thinkers such as Emerson, Thoreau, and Alcott. During this time he was able to write and publish, but was still not able to support his family, which by 1844 included a daughter. Poverty even forced the family to break up briefly.

In 1846 Hawthorne secured an appointment as Surveyor of the Custom House at Salem through the influence of his Bowdoin friend, Franklin Pierce. That same year a son was born, and Hawthorne was able to publish *Mosses from an Old Manse*. A change in administrations forced Hawthorne out of the post, freeing him to begin writing *The Scarlet Letter*. During this time he became friends with Herman Melville, who was writing *Moby Dick*.

In his years of reading, (supposedly, Hawthorne read almost every title and document in the Salem Antheneum) Hawthorne researched the role in history of his ancestors, the Judges Hathorne of Salem, who were among the original settlers of the colony. Judge Hathorne, the younger, had pronounced a sentence of death on several persons found guilty of witchcraft in the legendary Salem Witchcraft Trials.

Hawthorne also learned, through his reading of the historical and court documents of Salem and Boston, that a woman found guilty of adultery actually was sentenced to wearing a red letter "A" as a brand of her sinfulness. This information was the seed of a novel wherein Hawthorne tries to imagine the times when such a verdict would be possible and the sufferings of the people caught in such a harsh judgment.

The Scarlet Letter, published in 1850, was well-received, but again Hawthorne did not benefit financially to any great extent. Over the next few years, as the family moved from place to place, Hawthorne published *The House of the Seven Gables, The Blithedale Romance, A Wonder Book for Boys and Girls, Tanglewood Tales,* and *A Life of Pierce.* The last, a campaign biography for his former classmate, earned him an appointment as United States Consul at Liverpool, England.

As Consul in England, Hawthorne kept extensive notebooks during the years 1853 to 1857, but was unable to write any fiction. The next two years were spent in Italy where he began *The Marble Faun,* his last novel. In 1859 the family returned to England where Hawthorne published *The Marble Faun.* In 1860 the Hawthornes returned to the United States.

Hawthorne experienced failing health and was unable to complete any works over the next four years. He died on May 19, 1864 while on a brief vacation with Franklin Pierce.

Historical Background

The years in which Nathaniel Hawthorne lived and wrote were turbulent ones for the young nation. The country did share a cultural harmony based on strong community values linking hard work and virtue to success. In addition, the majority of citizens shared the idea that the United States, under divine guidance, was destined for greatness. Among the negatives, however, was the sense that some of the original values of the Revolution were being lost. Political reform movements sprang up. Utopian experiments were tried. New religious sects, unhappy with old theologies, broke away from the established churches. Over the course of Hawthorne's life, the United States was engaged in three wars, skirmishes with the Native American peoples, economic depressions, and problems with newly arriving immigrants. Looming large on the horizon and eventually leading to civil war was the conflict over slavery. Like that of many writers, Hawthorne's work reflects the times in which he lived.

The idea of writing as a career was also evolving. Increased literacy was creating a market for mass-produced books. Fiction became increasingly popular with readers, and the young nation was looking for writers who might compete on the cultural level of the Europeans. Writing became a way to possible fame and fortune. To be financially successful, however, a writer had to be very good and productive at his craft. Most writers had to work at occupations other than writing to support their families.

The Scarlet Letter was well received when it was published in 1850. It is one of those rare works which, recognized as a "classic" immediately upon publication, has remained in print and impressed generations of readers. Despite the desire of the reading public in 1850 for a balance of humor and pathos in new works, the publisher was enthusiastic over what Hawthorne thought to be a defect— *The Scarlet Letter* stressed the dark and somber side of human affairs.

The critics were nearly unanimous in their proclaiming *The Scarlet Letter* a major American novel. History has proven these critics right; *The Scarlet Letter* has never been out of print in its century-and-a-half existence. While very religious critics found his topic—a couple enmeshed in adultery—to be immoral, and Hawthorne's treatment of them too sympathetic, most commented on the novel's stylistic perfection, its intensity of effect, and its insight into the human soul. Hawthorne was quickly elevated to the position of the nation's foremost man of letters.

Master List of Characters

The narrator—*Though he does not participate in the plot, the narrator is a storyteller who presents various versions of events and, from the vantage point of 1850, comments on the characters and their actions.*

The people of Boston in the 1640s —*Puritan colonists who set out to purify their lives and who live under strict moral codes. They punish the adulteress, Hester Prynne, by making her continually wear a scarlet letter "A" as she lives among them.*

The town beadle —*A town official who leads Hester to the scaffold, the place of public punishment, and reads out her sentence.*

Hester Prynne—*A young Englishwoman who has given birth to a child out of wedlock and is now forced to wear the scarlet letter "A," publicly marking her as an adulteress. She refuses to make known the identity of the father.*

Pearl—*The daughter of Hester Prynne and her unknown lover; she brings both pleasure and pain to Hester.*

Roger Chillingworth—*The assumed name of Hester's husband who sent her ahead to Boston and who arrives to witness her disgrace and his. He is determined to find the identity of her lover and to exact his revenge. He has lived among the native peoples and learned their herbal medicines.*

The Reverend Mr. John Wilson—*The eldest clergyman of Boston who thinks highly of the Reverend Dimmesdale. He is concerned that Pearl be properly raised.*

Governor Bellingham—*The royal appointee who oversees the political needs of the colony.*

The Reverend Mr. Arthur Dimmesdale—*A young clergyman, who agonizes for many years over his real or imagined sinfulness and unworthiness.*

Master Brackett—*The jailer who summons Chillingworth to calm Hester and her child after the scaffold ordeal.*

Mistress Hibbins—*A sister of the governor and a reputed witch. She taunts both Hester and Dimmesdale about their secret.*

The sea captain—*A man known to Hester through her charity work. He agrees to take Hester, Pearl, and Dimmesdale from Salem to Bristol, England.*

Summary of the Novel

On a day in June 1642, the people of the Puritan colony of Boston await the public humiliation of a sinner among them. Hester Prynne is to stand on the scaffold in the village square for three hours. The red letter "A" which she has embroidered on her dress and the baby she holds in her arms brand her as an adulteress.

Hester refuses to name the father. Her husband, an old scholar, had sent her ahead two years earlier and is now in the crowd observing the scene. Under the guise of a medical doctor and the assumed name of Roger Chillingworth, Dr. Prynne demands unsuccessfully the name of the child's father and vows revenge on him.

Hester takes up residence with her daughter Pearl at the edge of the village. Chillingworth remains as the town physician and moves in with the young Reverend Dimmesdale, whose physical health is deteriorating but whose sermons about sin are more powerful than ever. Chillingworth determines that Dimmesdale is indeed the father of Pearl and torments the minister with innuendo and debate while keeping him alive with medicines. During this period Hester successfully rebuffs efforts to remove Pearl from her keeping.

For seven years, Hester suffers her outcast state until the deterioration of the minister's health forces her to confront him. Arthur Dimmesdale, her lover, and Hester meet in the forest where they renew their love and commitment and resolve to return to England together. However, the minister is unable to endure his spiritual agony and mounts the public scaffold in the dark of night, confessing his sin where no one can hear him. He is discovered by Hester and Pearl, and observed there by Chillingworth, who persuades him that his confession is a symptom of his illness.

The next morning, however, the minister leaves a public procession to mount the scaffold in the light of day. Joined by Hester and Pearl, and unsuccessfully restrained by Chillingworth, Dimmesdale confesses his guilt and dies. Chillingworth, now deprived of his life's purpose, dies within a year, leaving his fortune to Pearl. Mother and daughter leave Boston, but many years later, Hester returns to take up quiet residence and resume wearing the scarlet letter and doing good works.

Estimated Reading Time

Hawthorne prefaces his novel with an introductory essay entitled "The Custom-House" which an average reader could finish in an hour and ten minutes. If you are assigned the essay to read, Hawthorne's style and vocabulary level will probably require that you read the essay in two or three sittings, taking notes as you read. Compare your understanding to the summary and analysis in this *MAXnotes* volume.

Reading *The Scarlet Letter* by itself will require about ten hours for the average reader. Read the novel in its entirety or in sections as presented in this *MAXnotes* volume. Keep notes as you read and compare them to the summaries and comprehension questions that follow to confirm your understanding of ideas and events.

Hawthorne's novel consists of 24 chapters of various lengths. So that *The Scarlet Letter* may be more easily understood, the chapters have been grouped into sections and given titles which reflect the writer's focus in each section. Study questions and essay topics appear at the end of each section.

"The Custom-House"

(Essay)

Summary

To support himself and his family, the narrator accepted a presidential appointment in 1846 as the Surveyor, or overseer, of the custom-house for the port of Salem, Massachusetts. "The Custom-House" essay records the events and characters he encounters and their effect on his thinking, and can be closely linked to the novel. The first section addresses the reader, describes the Custom-House, and explores relationships to his ancestors and to Salem. The next section comments on the characters and the politics of his government job. The third section attempts to authenticate the novel as being based in historical fact and to show the novelist as merely an editor retelling another's story.

Hawthorne's descriptions of certain officers of the Custom-House as both lazy and mindless caused much criticism, and so he begins the second edition of the novel with a preface saying he feels "The Custom-House" was candid and in good humor, so he sees no need to apologize.

Hawthorne begins the essay itself with a description of the wharf in his native town of Salem. The Custom-House and its surroundings have seen busier times and are now in a state of disrepair. The American eagle emblem over the entrance serves as a metaphor for government service—those who seek security there, as he did, will eventually be cast out, a theme Hawthorne returns to later.

Hawthorne speaks with mixed feeling about his direct ancestors, William Hathorne and his son John, and their reputations as stern Puritans. Both are recorded as dealing especially harshly with women: John Hathorne was one of the judges at the Salem witch trials who never repented for his involvement. Both, he feels, would be upset to learn that a descendent of theirs was a mere "writer of story-books." Hawthorne feels it is good that a family be transplanted occasionally because of the difficulty of living up (or down) to the reputations of one's ancestors.

Determined as he was to live someplace other than Salem, Hawthorne feels a compulsion to return several times in his life. "This strange, indolent, unjoyous attachment" for his native town brings him back to accept the appointment overseeing the collections of tariffs.

The narrator speaks next of the politics of his appointment and of the characters who draw salaries at the Custom-House. The majority of the officeholders were Whigs and feared dismissal by a

Democrat. He fired only a few of the chronic no-shows and developed an easy tolerance for the remainder. The essay focuses on three characters in particular: the Inspector, the Collector, and the man of business.

The Inspector was the oldest and most worthless of the men drawing salaries from the government. His chief concern seemed to be dinner and the memory of dinners past. The narrator describes him as " . . . so shallow, so delusive, so impalpable, such an absolute nonentity. . . . My conclusion was that he had no soul, no heart, no mind. . . . "

While the Inspector's utter worthlessness as a worker and as a person astounded the narrator, another character's heroic countenance won his admiration. The Collector, General Miller, was a veteran of the War of 1812 and conducted himself with quiet elegance. The narrator compares him to Fort Ticonderoga, which, though in ruins, still showed the endurance, integrity, and benevolence of other, younger days.

The third person, the man of business, was an official so aptly suited for the demands of the Custom-House that the narrator called him " . . . the mainspring that kept its various wheels in motion." The narrator enjoyed the personalities he encountered and speculated whether a man of letters, such as he, could also be a man of business.

The narrator's intellectual curiosity led him to a storage room where, among the records of a Surveyor Pru, he found an embroidered piece of red cloth in the shape of the letter "A." He reports that when he placed it on his breast, he felt a burning sensation. An accompanying manuscript explained the history of the letter and of the woman, Hester Prynne, who had to wear it. The narrator felt charged by the ghost of Surveyor Pru to write the story of Hester Prynne but was unable to do any creative work while in government service.

The actual loss of his position with the return to power of the Whig party was devastating to Hawthorne. This loss is reflected in the narrator's feeling "decapitated" and betrayed, but he soon puts events in perspective and celebrates the return of his creative powers. The writer feels grateful for his experiences and takes leave of his readers.

Analysis

Beneath the surface of the narrator's reminiscences about his three years in government service and his supposed discovery of a tattered bit of red cloth, researchers have found much to help us interpret *The Scarlet Letter* with more confidence and to help us understand the writer with more insight. In addition to supposedly explaining the origin of the idea for *The Scarlet Letter*, "The Custom-House" allows scholars to explore the depths of Hawthorne and his novel.

One such understanding reached by many scholars is that the narrators of both works are the same man, and that understanding the tone and voice Hawthorne uses in his introductory essay gives insight into the novel. The narrator of "The Custom-House" is, in turn, haunted by his Puritan ancestors, awed by their accomplishments, uncertain whether they totally deserve the reputation that history records, shamed by their acts, and apologetic about his choice of careers. This complex set of reactions can be found in the narrator's descriptions of and comments about the Puritans of the novel and aid us as we decide whether the novel is a wholesale condemnation of Puritanism. The ancestors Hawthorne describes were probably the model for Puritan leaders in his novel.

Surprising parallels can be seen between the personal events Hawthorne tells of in the essay and his characters' lives in the novel. Like Hester, Hawthorne felt compelled to return to a place that was charged with infamy. He returns to Salem where his ancestors' reputations still affect the way people treat him; Hester returns to Boston to take up the shame of the scarlet letter. Like Hester, Hawthorne, in losing his government position, felt betrayed and abandoned. Like Dimmesdale, he felt powerless in his calling, and like the minister, felt a pain upon his breast—in Hawthorne's case, the "A" might stand for "art," his "idle passion." Like Dimmesdale, Hawthorne felt isolated and attempted to rejoin the larger world by speaking publicly about his private life. Like Chillingworth, Hawthorne has taken some revenge upon those who did not appreciate him—his characterizations of the government workers are insulting. All three characters are isolated from their fellow humans, a feeling echoed in Hawthorne's attempt to reestablish links to the public with his "autobiographical impulse."

Finding the original scarlet letter and Hester Prynne's history is a bit of dramatic fiction created by Hawthorne to give more authenticity to the tale of sin and punishment which follows the essay. He had written earlier of another woman character forced to undergo a similar punishment, and the fictional nature of this section, in which he feels a burning pain when he happens to place the red scrap of cloth on his chest, is readily apparent. Finding the records of Hester Prynne's supposed life establishes the narrator up as a reteller of history and allows him great leeway as he presents ideas and events.

A writer uses his own emotional life to more effectively create believable characters. Insights into the narrator and characters of the essay carry over to the novel. "The Custom-House" is a key to a deeper understanding of the novel, and a rereading of it after *The Scarlet Letter* will benefit the student with increased understanding of the novel, the essay, and the author himself.

Study Questions

1. What two reasons does Hawthorne give for writing "The Custom-House"?

2. What are the economic conditions at the port of Salem when Hawthorne becomes Surveyor of the Custom-House in 1846?

3. What does the American eagle over the entrance to the Custom-House represent according to the narrator?

4. What actions does the newly-appointed Surveyor take?

5. What did the narrator think his earliest ancestors in the colonies would say about his career as a writer?

6. The narrator describes three officials of the Custom-House in great detail. Tell who they were and describe the characteristics of each.

7. What did the narrator find in a storage room?

8. What does the narrator feel when he placed the found article on his chest?

9. What does the narrator contend is the effect on an individual of working for the government?

10. What were the narrator's reactions to losing his position as Surveyor in 1849?

Answers

1. Hawthorne wished to talk of "three years' experience in a Custom-House" and to authenticate the historical basis of *The Scarlet Letter*.

2. In 1846 Salem was no longer a bustling port. There was little work to be done.

3. After losing his job because a new president had been elected, he felt that the eagle represented only short-term security for those seeking a protected career. The eagle was very apt to kick its nestlings from the nest.

4. Instead of making great changes when he took over, the narrator settled into the slow routine of the Custom-House. During this time he made little attempt to write.

5. His stern, self-reliant ancestors would not approve of his being "a mere writer of storybooks."

6. One, the Inspector, is described as shallow, mindless, soulless, worthless as an employee, and concerned only with sensory gratification. The second, the Collector, is a veteran of great battles and responsibilities, heroic in character, a man of integrity, endurance, and benevolence. The third is a man described as ideally suited for the business of being a revenue collector, able to understand and handle all business situations.

7. While going through Surveyor Pru's desk, Hawthorne reports finding a scrap of red cloth and the history of Hester Prynne.

8. Hawthorne reports feeling a burning sensation in his chest.

9. He feels government service weakens a person's self reliance, a topic on which he and his Puritan ancestors could agree.

10. Although he is initially bitter about losing his job, the narrator rejoices that his impulse to write *The Scarlet Letter* has now been freed.

Suggested Essay Topics

1. How does Hawthorne feel about the Puritan attitudes of his ancestors, and why does he feel they would disapprove of his craft of fiction writing? How does Hawthorne portray these people? What about them does he dislike, and what does he admire?

2. Discuss Hawthorne's organizational style and sense of unity within "The Custom-House" essay.

SECTION THREE

Hester in Disgrace
(Chapters 1-4)

Chapter 1: "The Prison Door"

Summary

Our attention is focused on the door of Boston's prison-house on a day in June 1642. The building, a concession to the fact that crime exists even among a people dedicated to perfecting themselves, is itself very ugly. The only hint of beauty is a rose bush blooming at one side of the door. The narrator suggests that it sprang from the footstep of Anne Hutchinson, a woman persecuted for her religious beliefs and held in this same prison. The narrator further suggests the moral of his story, like the solitary rose, may be the only bright spot in the forthcoming tale of human sorrow.

Analysis

In this short opening chapter, Hawthorne dramatically sets the stage for the entrance of his main characters while also setting the tone for his story, "a tale of human frailty and sorrow" whose only bright spot is the moral lesson we may learn from it. Hawthorne was aware that readers of his times expected stories to be balanced with happiness and sadness, and he is preparing them for the tragic events about to unfold.

Chapter 2: "The Market-Place"

New Characters:

Women in the crowd: *Puritan women who comment on Hester's punishment*

The town beadle: *the official who publicly pronounces Hester's punishment*

Hester Prynne: *a young Englishwoman who, although her husband has been absent for two years, has given birth to a daughter*

Pearl: *Hester's infant daughter*

Summary

After the narrator tells of earlier punishments carried out upon the scaffold, our attention is focused upon several Puritan women in the waiting crowd and their reactions to Hester's punishment. One suggests that the women, if they had the power, would have given harsher judgments; another suggests a hot branding iron should be placed on Hester's forehead. A young wife suggests pity, but she is countered by another who demands Hester's death.

Hester is now led into the sunshine after her three-month im-
prisonment. She is carrying her
child and wearing a scarlet letter "A"
attached to her bodice with gold
embroidery. Her first impulse
seems to be to cower, but she walks
with grace and beauty to the scaffold and begins three hours of public humiliation. As she stands upon
the scaffold, her mind retraces her
life from a poverty-stricken child-
hood in England to her arranged
marriage to an old, misshapen

scholar, to her arrival alone in Salem, and to her present predicament.

Analysis

In Chapter 2, Hester, one of the main characters in the novel,
is shown as a person of sensitivity and pride. The scarlet letter
which she has been forced to wear has been attached with fanciful
gold embroidery, suggesting that a part of her rejects the shame
attached to it. Her walk to the scaffold suggests a strength of character which both astounds and infuriates many in the crowd. As
her memories are revealed, we begin to understand the forces
which have brought her to this moment.

A close reading of this section reveals much about Puritan attitudes and about Hawthorne's attitude toward them. The majority of women in the crowd want a harsher judgment imposed upon
Hester, while the town beadle proclaims the virtue of a society in
which sin was exposed and punished. Hawthorne, though he char-
acterizes the Puritans as coarse and unyielding, shows them to be
acting for the good of the group and in accord with their beliefs.
They contrast favorably in his eyes with later society which has
" . . . grown corrupt enough to smile, instead of shuddering" at a
person's guilt and shame.

Chapter 3: "The Recognition"

New Characters:

Dr. Roger Chillingworth: *Hester Prynne's husband who had sent her ahead to Salem. He has been shipwrecked and held hostage by the Indians for nearly two years. Dr. Prynne assumes the name of Chillingworth when he sees his wife being punished for adultery*

Governor Bellingham: *political leader of Salem*

The Reverend Mister Wilson: *eldest clergyman of Salem who wishes Hester to reveal the identity of the father*

The Reverend Mister Dimmesdale: *young minister who has had an affair with Hester Prynne*

Summary

From the scaffold Hester recognizes someone on the edge of the crowd. Her husband, who has been held hostage by the Indians, has arrived at the settlement to be ransomed. He now recognizes his wife, whom he signals to be quiet. Through conversation with a man from the town, Dr. Prynne learns that the identity of the father of Hester's child is still unknown. He vows to find the man's identity and make it known.

Near the end of her three-hour stay upon the scaffold, the authorities direct Hester to reveal the father's identity. The Reverend John Wilson is first to demand she cooperate, noting that the young Reverend Dimmesdale was opposed to forcing Hester to speak out. Governor Bellingham joins Wilson in beseeching Dimmesdale to convince Hester to speak. Dimmesdale delivers an impassioned plea to Hester to consider her actions and how they might affect the father, who may not himself have the courage to confess his sin. Hester refuses to name the father and, after enduring an hour-long sermon by Reverend Wilson, is led back with her crying child to the prison. Several report seeing the scarlet letter cast a lurid gleam as she walks through the dark passageway.

Analysis

Chapter 3 introduces the remaining major characters, Roger Chillingworth and Arthur Dimmesdale. Hester's husband, who will later be known as Dr. Roger Chillingworth, arrives in the settlement dressed in a mixture of savage and civilized garb, perhaps symbolic of his nature. He hides his true identity and shows himself to be a man who can mask his inner turmoil as well. His effect upon Hester is striking; we are told she would rather stand in public shame than meet with him privately.

Several references to Dimmesdale have already suggested that he is the father whose identity is being sought: he is reported to have been very disturbed at Hester's situation, he has argued against forcing her to confess, and ironically, he is named by Wilson as the person with whom " . . . the responsibility of this woman's soul lies greatly. . . . " In this first of the novel's three scaffold scenes, Dimmesdale, located above her on the balcony with the other revered authorities, makes a plea to Hester to reveal the father but also to consider her actions carefully. If he is speaking of himself when he speaks of the other sinner, Dimmesdale is admitting that he has not the courage to confess. Part of him envies Hester for not evading public humiliation, while part of him is afraid she will reveal his guilt to the townspeople.

Reporting that some had observed the scarlet letter glowing introduces a supernatural element to the scene, suggesting that the story will be more than a mere retelling of history.

Chapter 4: "The Interview"

New Character:

Master Brackett: *the jailer*

Summary

Hester and her child are visibly upset when they are returned to the prison, and Master Brackett decides they would benefit from a doctor's care. Now living within the jail while the authorities pay his ransom to the Indians is such a man, Roger Chillingworth.

When left alone with Hester and her child, he gives a potion to

calm the child. Hester drinks a potion herself after hearing Chillingworth say that he could wish no better vengeance upon than she wear the scarlet letter for the rest of her life. Chillingworth accepts part of the blame for their shame; he, a misshapen scholar, should not have married such a young and passionate woman. They agree that each has wronged the other.

Chillingworth pressures Hester to reveal the identity of the father and, when she refuses, vows to find him. Hester is sworn to keep Chillingworth's true identity a secret so that he may move more easily about the settlement to find the guilty party. He also wants to avoid the shame of having an unfaithful wife.

Analysis

"The Interview" reveals Chillingworth to have a reasonable side to his nature. He may be angry but he will not revenge himself upon the innocent child or a woman already being punished—in fact, he takes a portion of the blame for Hester's disgrace upon himself for thinking that he, an old and deformed intellectual, could marry one so young and have a normal family life. Hester's promise to keep his identity secret sets up one of the major conflicts of the novel: Chillingworth's revenge upon the man who has disgraced him. This revenge is possible only because Hester agrees to keep the secret. As the chapter concludes, Hester mentally compares his expression to that of the devil while Chillingworth focuses on what is to become his life's objective—revenge.

Study Questions

1. What is the setting of the story?
2. What legend accounts for the existence of the rose bush by the prison door?
3. What is the mood of the crowd, and why is their attention focused on the door?
4. What reasons are given as to why Hester Prynne was not executed for her crime? What would the Puritan women have done to her if given the power?
5. What are Hester's specific actions as she walks from the prison to the scaffold?
6. What memories does Hester review during her three-hour ordeal?
7. Tell where each of the following are located while Hester is on the scaffold: her daughter Pearl, the Reverend Mr. Dimmesdale, and her former husband, Roger Chillingworth.
8. What specifically is Dimmesdale's plea to Hester?

9. During their interview, what is Chillingworth's attitude toward Hester and her act of infidelity?

10. What promise does Chillingworth exact from Hester?

Answers

1. *The Scarlet Letter* is set in the Puritan colony of Salem, Massachusetts during the 1640s. Specifically, the action begins in the market-place of Salem on a morning in June 1642.

2. The rose bush was said to have grown out of the footsteps of Anne Hutchinson. She was a heretic who taught that personal faith was superior to the force of moral law. The Puritans imprisoned her, then drove her from the colony.

3. Most of the crowd are serious and somber, as if they were about to witness an execution. They are waiting to witness the public humiliation of an adulterer among them.

4. The men governing the colony feel that Hester Prynne is young and fair and therefore more likely than most to give in to temptation. Moreover, her husband may very well be dead. The majority of women want Hester to be branded on her forehead or even put to death.

5. Hester shrugs off the beadle's hand on her shoulder, pauses a moment outside the door of the prison, and looks around at the townspeople. She resists the urge to cover the scarlet letter with the baby she is carrying, and walks serenely and gracefully to the scaffold.

6. During the three hours on the scaffold Hester remembers a decaying ancestral home, the parents who loved her, her marriage to a pale, thin, misshapen scholar, and life in the capitals of Europe with the old scholar.

7. Pearl is in Hester's arms, Dimmesdale is above Hester on a balcony of the meeting-house, and Chillingworth is on the edge of the crowd gathered in the market-place.

8. Dimmesdale says that Hester must realize the pressure he is under. If she feels it is the right thing to do, she should re-

veal the name of the father. Doing so would be for his own good, even if he were to come down from a high place, since he probably does not have the courage to do so himself. He is greatly relieved when Hester refuses to answer.

9. Chillingworth feels the scale is balanced between them; she should not have committed adultery, while he should not have married so young and vibrant a girl and left her alone. He seeks no revenge on Hester.

10. Hester promises to keep her husband's identity a secret.

Suggested Essay Topics

1. Describe the narrator of the story. How does the narrator differ from a traditional first- or third-person narrator?

2. Discuss the beadle as the personification of Puritan thinking.

Hester in the Community
(Chapters 5–8)

Chapter 5: "Hester at her Needle"

Summary

After her ordeal upon the scaffold, Hester Prynne, free to leave the colony, chooses to remain and takes up residence in an abandoned cottage on the outskirts of the town. To support herself and her child, Hester becomes a seamstress, famous for her needlework, though she is not allowed to sew wedding garments.

Wearing the scarlet letter has several effects upon her. Even as Hester does charity work, she has to endure insults from the poor and the sick she is helping. She finds herself often at the center of sermons and public lectures and jeers. Sensing different reactions from certain men and women, she imagines the letter has given her the power to see the hidden sins of others.

Analysis

This chapter is the first of several throughout the book in which Hawthorne focuses on a single character or relationship without using dialogue or advancing the plot very much. Here the first three

years of Hester's predicament are summarized.

The narrator suggests that Hester remains in Salem for three reasons: she feels compelled to stay in the place where a great event marked her life; she is closer to the man who fathered her child; and lastly, she feels that " . . . here . . . had been the scene of her guilt, and here should be the scene of her earthly punishment."

While Hester's skill at the needle fills a need within the community and allows her to perform charity work as penance, she is continually isolated and punished by the community, a situation she accepts quietly. Hester stops short of praying for her tormentors, afraid that her prayers might turn into curses.

Chapter 6: "Pearl"

New Character:

Pearl: *Hester's perplexing child*

Summary

The narrator devotes this chapter to the first three years of Pearl's life, so named because she cost her mother "a great price" (a Biblical reference). She is a child with no apparent physical defect but one who has moods of defiance and gloom mixed with great exuberance. In public, Pearl acts as if she were a child of the devil, defiantly hurling stones at the other Puritan children. Privately, Hester at first thought Pearl might be a fairy child because of her wild swings of mood. Hester later saw in Pearl's eyes the image of an evil spirit.

Pearl has been fascinated by the scarlet letter upon her mother's bosom. One afternoon she pelts the spot with wildflowers while Hester endures the emotional pain. In a discussion of her origin, Pearl declares she has no heavenly father.

Analysis

Pearl seems to be the living embodiment of the scarlet letter. She is beautiful, just as the embroidered letter is, yet she brings her mother much pain. Within her personality are the mixed emotions that are contained within the letter—defiance, gloom, shame, and anger. She is as uncontrollable as the situation that the letter represents.

The devil is a continuing presence in the story, showing himself as The Black Man in the Forest, in the fiendish look of Chillingworth during the meeting in prison, and now in the form of Pearl, the devil-child. Pearl senses the pain the scarlet letter causes her mother and torments her about it with words and deeds.

Note that these conclusions about Pearl's being an imp or demon-child are made through the eyes of the Puritans, who are biased towards her, and through the eyes of Hester, the adulterous mother who feels the guilt of bringing Pearl into the world and is

reluctant to discipline the child. Pearl functions in the story on three levels: as a real child, as a continuing symbol of Hester and Dimmesdale's adultery, and as an allegorical figure sent to torment the sinners and direct their actions.

Chapter 7: "The Governor's Hall"

Summary

Hester has heard that Governor Bellingham is considering removing Pearl from her care. There have been rumors that Pearl is of demon origin and that she would be better raised by someone more respectable than Hester. Hester hopes to convince the Governor to allow her to keep the child.

Pearl stands out from the other children because Hester has taken to dressing her in scarlet trimmed in fancy gold embroidery_ the scarlet letter in another form. On their way to see the Governor, they are accosted by children hurling mud and insults. Pearl drives them off, and the two continue on.

A servant informs them that Governor Bellingham is conferring with one or two ministers and a doctor. While they wait, Pearl points to polished armor and notes the exaggerated proportions the surface gives to her mother's scarlet letter. The Governor and three visitors then approach them from the garden as the chapter ends.

Analysis

Themes and character traits noted in earlier chapters are continued here. Pearl is a demon-child and should be treated differently. Hester is not a person to be given any moral responsibility. Pearl, dressed in scarlet, represents the scarlet letter, in form and in spirit, as she finds little ways to pain her mother with references to the letter. Hester shows strength and determination as she faces the authorities.

An additional focus of the chapter is the lush furnishings of Governor Bellingham's mansion. In contrast to the sparse lifestyle of the Puritans, the authorities lived in surroundings which imitated as much as possible the great houses of England. Spacious halls, sparkling stucco exteriors, and many windows gave a cheeriness that ordinary Puritans would have avoided.

Chapter 8:
"The Elf-Child and the Minister"

New Character:

Mistress Hibbins: *sister of the Governor, reputed to be a witch*

Summary

Governor Bellingham is the first of the group to come upon Pearl and expresses surprise at her brightly colored outfit. Reverend Wilson is next to react and asks if she is a Christian child. Wilson then recognizes Hester Prynne and tells Bellingham that this is the woman and child of whom they were just speaking.

The Governor explains that for the sake of Pearl's soul, the authorities are considering removing her from Hester's care and raising her more strictly. When Hester replies that she can better teach morality to the child because of what she has learned from the scarlet letter, they decide to question the child to see if she has been reared properly.

Pearl refuses to cooperate at first with the questioning, but finally answers Wilson's question, " . . . who made thee?" Though she has been taught the correct answers to all these questions of the catechism (religious instruction), Pearl replies that she had not been made but had been plucked by her mother off the bush that grew by the prison door. When the Governor says that the decision to taken Pearl away from Hester is obvious, Hester replies that Pearl is both her happiness and her torture and that she cannot lose her. She turns to Dimmesdale and demands that he intervene with the authorities. He does so, arguing that Pearl's presence also serves to save the mother's soul which might otherwise be lost to Satan.

Chillingworth, whom Hester noted to have grown uglier in the intervening three years, comments on Dimmesdale's earnest plea and joins in asking that Pearl remain with Hester. It is decided that Pearl will be taught directly by one of the ministers and that she will be supervised at school and at church meetings.

While the conversation goes on, Dimmesdale steps back a bit. Pearl, observed only by her mother, spontaneously goes to him and puts her cheek against his hand. As Pearl runs off, Wilson speculates that she may well be a witch. Chillingworth wonders whether analyzing the child's nature could lead to the identity of the father, but he is warned by Reverend Dimmesdale to avoid such "profane philosophy" and either to pray about it or to let Providence take its course.

The narrator tells us that one version of the story reports that Hester, as she is leaving, is invited by Mistress Hibbins to join other witches in the forest that night, an invitation that Hester says she might have accepted if the authorities had not allowed her to keep Pearl.

Analysis

The opening paragraphs of this chapter confirm that the ruling authorities had a taste for the good things in life, while their concern for Pearl's salvation shows that they considered such a decision to be very important. When Pearl behaves poorly and Hester realizes she in danger of losing her, Hester turns to Dimmesdale. When it is clear to Dimmesdale that Hester will do anything to keep Pearl, including revealing the father's identity, he responds with an earnest and successful plea to the Governor.

Pearl's response that she had been plucked from the bush that grew by the prison door is true in one sense. She is the offspring of a radical thinker just as the blooms by the prison could be symbolically said to be the offspring of Anne Hutchinson, alluded to in Chapter 1. Hutchinson's doctrine of faith over obedience to the moral law caused her to be driven from the colony. Hawthorne uses this opportunity to tie Hester to other women who philosophically opposed the strict controls of Puritan society.

The interlude between Pearl and Dimmesdale illustrates Hawthorne's idea that people who have connections between them will have sympathetic responses to each other. Here, Pearl intuitively responds to her father. Earlier, Hester felt she could recognize others who had sinned, while Chillingworth foretold that he would be able to recognize the man who wronged him.

A stylistic device within the novel is the writer's use of several versions of the same episode. Did Mistress Hibbins actually invite Hester to join with the devil in the forest? Did the scarlet letter itself cast a gleam in the dark passageway of the prison? This presenting of alternate versions gives an air of credibility to the narrator as he attempts to present us with as much "truth" as possible. This writing device also allows Hawthorne to suggest supernatural explanations for events in his novel without losing readers who might reject a story totally based in the supernatural.

Study Questions

1. After her ordeal, where did Hester choose to live? Why?

2. What occupation did Hester take up?

3. Describe Hester's appearance and mental state during this time period.

4. Give at least three examples of Hester's treatment by the community.

5. Describe Pearl's personality and appearance.

6. What is Pearl's reaction to the scarlet letter?

7. Why does Hester go the Governor's house?

8. Describe the luxury of the Governor's home, especially in contrast to an ordinary Puritan's lifestyle.

9. How does Pearl behave when questioned by the men?

10. How does Hester succeed in her mission, and how does this relate to her conversation with Mistress Hibbins?

Answers

1. Free to go anywhere, Hester remains in Salem, taking up residence in an abandoned cottage on the outskirts of the community. She does so because she feels connected to Salem by her sin and because she feels linked to the man who was her lover.

2. Hester's ability to sew, shown by her embroidering of the scarlet letter itself, allows her to support herself. She sews everything from funeral shrouds to fancy apparel for the upper class.

3. On the outside Hester exhibits the somber manner the Puritans demand of her. She wears drab and coarse clothing and interacts with the community only in her work and in her charitable acts. Her passionate nature is hidden and redirected into her embroidery. Inwardly, she feels isolated and lonely but accepts this as her lot.

4. Everyone, rich and poor, makes comments to Hester about her sin. Clergymen preach sermons about her behavior. Children, imitating their parents' behavior, taunt her in the streets. Strangers, unaware of her situation, stare in puzzlement at her.

5. Pearl is described as wild, defiant, moody, exuberant, undisciplined, perceptive, and perverse. Hester dresses her in colorful outfits, beautifully embroidered, but is unable to control the actions of her young daughter who remains isolated from other children.

6. Even in her crib Pearl seemed fascinated with the scarlet letter. She grabbed on to it once and smiled, causing her mother considerable anguish. Pearl constantly smiles knowingly at the letter, renewing Hester's anguish each time she observes her child's sly smile. Once Pearl smilingly pelted the scarlet letter with flowers, an action her mother silently endured.

7. Hester has heard rumors that she is considered an unfit mother for so undisciplined a child. Since Pearl is the source of her joy as well as her torment, Hester is determined to keep her.

8. The Governor's mansion is described as large and airy with much sunshine coming through many windows. The outside, made of stucco mixed with glass, sparkles in the sunlight. The mansion is furnished with curtains and wall decorations, few of which would please an ordinary Puritan who lived a simple and unadorned life.

9. Pearl first jumps up on the window ledge, then puts her finger in her mouth, refusing to speak. She gives a seemingly nonsensical answer to a question from the catechism, though she knew the expected response from Hester's teaching.

10. Hester demands that Dimmesdale intercede for her. She implies that she will do anything to keep Pearl, including revealing that Dimmesdale is the father of the child. Hester, in reply to Hibbins' request that she join the Black Man in the Forest that night, replies that she would have done so if she had not won the right to Pearl.

Sample Essay Topics

1. Discuss the effect of the punishment upon Hester's personality.

2. Explore the relationship of the Governor's mansion to the "old world" and to the Puritans.

3. Examine some of the many symbols surrounding Hester Prynne, including the scarlet letter, her apparel, and her occupation.

Chillingworth and Dimmesdale

(Chapters 9–12)

Chapter 9: "The Leech"

Summary

Although not religious by nature, Roger Chillingworth chooses the Reverend Mr. Dimmesdale as his spiritual advisor, a choice designed to pique the reader's curiosity. Dimmesdale's humility and his many fasts and vigils have impressed the townspeople with his holiness, but they fear that his deteriorating physical condition has brought him close to death. The elders persuade him to seek the advice of the learned doctor. Though Dimmesdale says he prefers death to Chillingworth's medicines, he and the doctor spend long hours together talking about many subjects. To allow him to "help" the minister even more, Chillingworth arranges that the two of them should lodge in separate apartments at the home of a widow.

The narrator tells us that people of the town have differing opinions of the arrangement. Many see it as the answer to their prayers that the minister might be helped. Others see the new closeness as mysterious; rumors surface of Chillingworth's involvement with a conjurer in England and of his taking part in magic

rituals while a captive of the Indians. Most agree that his Chillingworth's expression has grown uglier and more evil since he moved in with the minister.

Analysis

The word "leech" refers here to a doctor because doctors used leeches to draw out "bad" blood from their patients. The appropriate double meaning of this word is apparent when we realize that Chillingworth has attached himself to the young minister and is slowly drawing out information from his troubled soul. Hawthorne's technique of offering different opinions of an event or character leads the reader to view Chillingworth as someone demonic and to see the main characters as taking part in a cosmic interplay of good and evil.

Chapter 10: "The Leech and His Patient"

Summary

Roger Chillingworth, described as a kindly man earlier in his life, is now described as a man possessed by a terrible fascination with Dimmesdale's secrets. During a conversation with the minister about strange plants he had found growing over a grave, Chillingworth remarks that perhaps they grew from a heart buried with some hideous secret—thus suggesting that he knows Dimmesdale himself hides a poisonous secret. Dimmesdale answers that there are many people with such secrets that they dare not reveal. Their conversation is interrupted by Pearl's laughter outside their open window. The doctor observes the girl sticking burrs from plants in the graveyard onto her mother's scarlet letter, an act which Hester endures quietly. Chillingworth wonders about the child's personality, and Dimmesdale offers that her personality is the result of a "broken law." Pearl throws a burr at Dimmesdale through the open window and runs away shouting that the Black Man has hold of the minister.

The conversation returns to the idea of hidden guilt bringing more pain than publicly acknowledged guilt. Chillingworth raises the idea of physical illness being caused by a spiritual disorder and asks Dimmesdale what he is withholding. The minister refuses further discussion and rushes from the room.

Later, after the two have re-established their superficial friendship, Chillingworth comes upon the minister asleep in a chair. He quickly uncovers Dimmesdale's chest and is greatly surprised and delighted at what he finds there.

Analysis

Chillingworth is using every opportunity to force the minister into an action or statement which will reveal him as Hester's lover. Using Pearl's comments and Hester's presence outside their window, he focuses the discussion on the minister's emotional trouble, saying it may well be causing the physical deterioration in Dimmesdale that has everyone concerned. This discussion of psychosomatic illness, a concept not accepted until many years later, is an excellent illustration of Hawthorne's ability to explore and present human psychology in readable form. The novel itself is a psychological and allegorical attempt to show the effects of sin upon personality.

The minister's rush from the room convinces Chillingworth that Dimmesdale has a rash, passionate side to his personality, showing him capable of committing adultery. Dimmesdale's habit of clutching his breast when he is distressed prompts the doctor to examine the area. We are not told what Chillingworth finds there, but the mark or condition seems to confirm that the doctor has found the man who has wronged him. Most readers assume that a scarlet letter "A" has erupted over the minister's heart.

Chapter 11: "The Interior of a Heart"

Summary

Certain that he had found out the identity of Hester's lover, Chillingworth now decides that public exposure of Dimmesdale is not as good a revenge as continued emotional torture. His comments are causing much pain to Dimmesdale, but the minister, focused as he is on his own sin, does not suspect Chillingworth's intentions.

The minister's sense of his own sin and the pain it continually causes has transformed him into a powerful and much revered preacher. While he painfully tells himself of his unworthiness and punishes himself with vigils and fasts, the congregation thinks him to be the model of holiness. Many times Dimmesdale resolves publicly to confess his sin but is only able to state from the pulpit how utterly worthless and vile a liar he is, confessions which only make him seem holier and humbler than the ordinary person.

Privately, Dimmesdale continues to punish himself with whippings and long periods of watching and fasting. On one such night vigil, a new idea, one which may bring him a moment's peace, occurs to him.

Analysis

Chillingworth is now certain that Dimmesdale is the man he seeks and realizes that he can derive more pleasure from continually torturing the minister with well-directed comments, a more

evil form of revenge. The minister's sincere humility and his attempts to confess his guilt ironically win him wide admiration as a
holy man, admiration that hurts him even more because he considers himself so undeserving. He punishes himself physically and
emotionally until suffering becomes his only "real existence on this
earth."

Chapter 12: "The Minister's Vigil"

Summary

On this May night the minister carries out the plan which oc-
curred to him in Chapter 11. He will stand on the scaffold, the place
of public humiliation on which Hester herself stood some seven
years before. The dark of the night hides him, and he believes the
town to be asleep. As he dwells on his sin and on the pain that
comes from whatever is on his chest, he shrieks aloud. The only
people who seem disturbed by his outburst are Bellingham and
Mistress Hibbins, but their lights are soon extinguished.

In the relative calm that returns, Dimmesdale observes a person carrying a lantern on the street by the scaffold. Recognizing
The Reverend Mr. Wilson, he boldly calls out to him but is not heard.
A new fear arises: he will be unable to move his stiff body from the
spot and will be discovered by the townspeople in the morning.
He laughs aloud at the thought and is surprised to hear childish
laughter answer his.

Hester explains that she and Pearl and others have been keeping a deathbed watch with Governor Winthrop and that she is going home to sew his shroud. Dimmesdale invites them to join him
on the scaffold, and, as they join hands, he feels a vital warmth, a
rush of new life. To Pearl's insistence that he stand with them at
noon of the following day, the minister replies that only on judgment day will they stand together. As he is speaking, the sky is lit
up by a giant meteor streaking across the sky. Its light reveals the
minister standing with his hand over his heart, Hester with her
scarlet letter, and Pearl, the embodiment of the scarlet letter, as
the link between them.

The narrator tells of ancient interpretations of such celestial events as having been divinely inspired. Dimmesdale imagines the meteor to have taken the shape of an immense letter "A," another symbol of his guilt.

The light of the meteor reveals another figure in the scene. Roger Chillingworth, returning from attending to the dying governor, has observed the three upon the scaffold and now offers to escort the minister home and out of the damp night air, pretending to believe the minister's odd vigil to be only a symptom of his illness.

Dimmesdale's sermon the next day is deemed the most powerful he has ever delivered. Afterwards, the sexton, a church official, returns Dimmesdale's glove, said to have been found on the scaffold, no doubt put there by the devil to discredit the minister. He speaks also of a meteor in the shape of the letter "A" observed last night and says that most have interpreted it as standing for "Angel" since the governor died that very night.

Analysis

After several chapters of background and generalities about the major characters, the action of the plot advances quickly. Dimmesdale's urge to stand on the scaffold begins a series of strange occurrences. The coincidences of the night—the death of the governor, the passing of the main characters by the scaffold, the outbursts which bring Hester and Pearl to the scaffold, and the bright momentary light of the meteor which has revealed the people on the scaffold to Chillingworth and the doctor to them, combine to push Dimmesdale closer to a possible public confession. The mention of the pain on his breast with other manifestations of the scarlet letter "A" strongly suggests that he carries such a letter carved or burned into his flesh, either self-inflicted or caused by divine action or emotional stress. Hawthorne does a good job here of reproducing Dimmesdale's psychotic thoughts and actions in an understandable way.

This scaffold scene is the second of three in the novel. Dimmesdale, although standing there under the cover of night, is now found upon the place of punishment embracing Hester and Pearl while Chillingworth comes closer. The momentary flash of

light can be interpreted as bringing Dimmesdale a step closer to full public disclosure.

Dimmesdale's interpreting the meteor's shape as a symbol of adultery is presented as a reflection of his confused emotional state. That the townspeople interpret it as a religious symbol may be an attempt to link them with the more primitive peoples the narrator speaks of earlier in the chapter.

Study Questions

1. What are the townspeople's reactions to Chillingworth's lodging in the same house as Dimmesdale?

2. What changes have taken place in Chillingworth over the years?

3. What actions does Dimmesdale take to punish himself?

4. Why is Chillingworth called a "leech," and why, at another point, does the narrator compare him to a miner?

5. What is the significance of Chillingworth's examining Dimmesdale's chest?

6. What is the reaction of Dimmesdale's parishioners to his sermons?

7. For what reasons are the major characters at the scaffold during the night?

8. Why does Dimmesdale cry out while on the scaffold?

9. Where is each major character located when the meteor is seen?

10. What are the various interpretations the characters attribute to the shape of the meteor?

Answers

1. Many are happy that a doctor will be close at hand to tend to their beloved minister. It is seen as the answer to their prayers. Others begin to notice changes in Chillingworth's appearance and personality, and rumors circulate that he might be in league with the devil. If there is any conflict between Chillingworth and Dimmesdale, they are sure the goodness in Dimmesdale will win out.

2. There was something ugly and evil in his face. It was widely held that he was the devil or the devil's agent come to persecute Dimmesdale.

3. Over the years Dimmesdale has taken to whipping his shoulders with a scourge, fasting until weak with hunger, and stay-

ing awake in night-long vigils.

4. Doctors used leeches to draw out bad blood, and the ironic use here is appropriate. Chillingworth is also presented as someone who was entering into the interior of a heart and digging, like a miner, to take out something precious.

5. Dimmesdale often clutches his chest and to this point has not allowed Chillingworth, his doctor, to examine him. Since Chillingworth suspects the minister has committed the same sin as Hester, it follows that he might be pained symbolically and literally in the same spot as she.

6. Ironically, the more earnestly Dimmesdale tells them that he is a sinner, the more powerful his sermons are to those who see him as the model of virtue. If this saintly man has sinned, they must be very unworthy of God's blessing.

7. Dimmesdale feels he might have more peace within himself if he stands at the place of atonement even though it is under the cover of night. The others are passing by after leaving the deathbed of Governor Winthrop: Hester as a nurse and shroud maker, Pearl as her companion, and Chillingworth as his doctor.

8. Dimmesdale shrieks out of horror at the thought that his guilt is exposed to the view of the universe. He calls to Wilson out of a fatalistic impulse that tells him he will soon be exposed because he feels he cannot move.

9. Dimmesdale, Hester, and Pearl are on the scaffold while Chillingworth is approaching it.

10. Dimmesdale interprets the shape to indicate that Heaven has taken notice of his guilt. The townspeople interpret the "A" to stand for "Angel" for the taking into heaven of Governor Winthrop.

Sample Essay Topics

1. Compare and contrast the effects of sin upon Arthur Dimmesdale and Roger Chillingworth.

2. Examine the strange relationship between Chillingworth and Dimmesdale.

3. Discuss Hawthorne's use of coincidence and irony in these chapters.

Changes in Hester

(Chapters 13–15)

Chapter 13: "Another View of Hester"

Summary

Seven years have passed since Pearl's birth. Hester is shocked at the poor physical and psychological state of Dimmesdale and resolves to do something to help his condition. Hester herself has been accepted by the community and has outwardly accepted the role she has been forced to assume. She has submitted uncomplainingly to menial tasks, to poor living conditions, and to public insults. Her charity and unfailing tenderness have earned her respect, and now most townspeople interpret the "A" upon her breast as standing for "Able."

Inwardly, though, Hester is not the model citizen she is thought to be. The letter seems to have stolen her youth and beauty while forcing her to develop an inner strength few others could understand. She speculates on the status of women in society and what changes must occur if they are ever to achieve equality. She accepts the consequences of her actions, but she will not accept the guilt that the scarlet letter was intended to have imbued her with.

Assessing Dimmesdale's deteriorating state and his continuing torture by Chillingworth, Hester resolves to confront her former husband. Soon she and Pearl meet Chillingworth on an isolated part of the seashore.

Analysis

The changes in Hester over the seven years since she first stood on the scaffold are remarkable. She has changed the attitudes of the people around her with her public demeanor while developing internal standards that have little to do with the Puritan community. Isolation from the community has allowed her to speculate on ideas others would not consider. The narrator presents her as a more modern woman, one of the age where old traditions and narrow patterns of thinking are falling away.

Hester's speculation allows the narrator to present an analysis of the place of women in American society both at the time the story takes place and at the time the story is being written, 1850. Through Hester he presents three steps which must occur before women achieve equality: the whole of society must be torn down and built anew, men must change their attitudes toward women, and women must change their image of themselves, perhaps losing their "ethereal essence," or femininity, as they do so. Hawthorne's blueprint for change shows remarkable perception of sociological currents in both societies.

Hester has also developed a strength of personality Dimmesdale cannot find within himself. She feels that she has grown and climbed to a higher point. Chillingworth has lowered himself by exacting revenge upon Dimmesdale. She is prepared to do whatever she can to help Dimmesdale.

Chapter 14: "Hester and the Physician"

Summary

While Pearl plays in a tidal pool, Hester speaks with Chillingworth, who has been gathering plants for his medicines. When Chillingworth tells her that the magistrates are considering allowing Hester to remove the scarlet letter, Hester replies that they do not have the power to remove it. She stares at the changes that seven years of seeking revenge have caused in Chillingworth. She goes on to speak of Dimmesdale and of her promise not to reveal her husband's identity to her lover. When Hester says that the doctor has exacted enough revenge, Chillingworth argues that he has kept Dimmesdale from the gallows, that he has kept the man, whose body lacked the spirit to withstand the pressures, alive. Here, as Chillingworth becomes very animated speaking of the years of revenge, he himself sees more clearly what he has become: a fiend whose only reason for being is revenge. Hester makes it plain that she will tell Dimmesdale the true identity of the doctor. She challenges her former husband to pardon Dimmesdale. He replies that he cannot—they are fated to play out their roles.

Analysis

Both characters seem to accept fate, but to different degrees. Chillingworth feels he does not have the power to forgive Dimmesdale, that the minister owes him even more since the man is responsible in Chillingworth's eyes for transforming him from a kindly scholar into a vengeance-seeking fiend. They are destined to continue as they are. Hester accepts her fate when she says that no one has the power to remove the scarlet letter from her while rejecting the idea that she is powerless. Dimmesdale's continued suffering is intolerable, and she will act to change the situation.

Chapter 15: "Hester and Pearl"

Summary

As Hester watches Chillingworth walk away gathering herbs, she marvels at his ugliness and involuntarily admits that she hates him. Memories of their marriage lead her to conclude that the wrong he did her, marrying a girl so young, was far greater than any wrong she did him.

Pearl has been playing nearby and now creates a letter "A" out of seagrass and places it on her chest. Hester, calling to her, notes the green letter and asks whether Pearl knows why her mother wears her letter. Pearl replies that all she knows is that it is for the same reason that the minister places his hand over his heart. She thinks that the reason might be known to the old doctor. Hester is tempted to take Pearl into her confidence and tell her the importance of the scarlet letter, but instead tells her child that the letter has no great importance. Pearl is not satisfied with this answer and pesters her mother until Hester threatens to put her in a dark closet.

Analysis

Hester undergoes several dramatic changes in this chapter. First, she permits herself to express her hatred for her former husband. In a reversal of her earlier position she now feels that she has suffered the greater wrong by being coerced into marriage with Chillingworth. Next, Hester sees a thoughtful side to her daughter's personality and speculates whether a new relationship with her is possible. Could a thoughtful young woman grow out of this impish child? Finally, to stop Pearl's pestering about the origin of the scarlet letter, Hester responds with a threat that silences the child, something she has had very little success at previously.

Study Questions

1. What are the effects of the letter on Hester Prynne over this seven year interval?

2. What crime has Hester committed which, if known to the Puritans, would have resulted in her death?

3. What value does Hester place upon her life?

4. What does Hester see as necessary before women would be treated equally in society?

5. What is the meaning of the line, "the scarlet letter had not done its office"?

6. Why does Hester feel responsible for Dimmesdale's physical condition?

7. What favors does Chillingworth feel he has done for Dimmesdale?

8. Why is Chillingworth even more vengeful towards Dimmesdale?

9. When is Hester untrue to the scarlet letter?

10. What is the current relationship between Hester and Pearl?

Answers

1. Her quiet acceptance of her status and her charity work have won her respect. The scarlet letter is now said to stand for "Able" and is even said by some to have a supernatural power to protect the wearer, but the letter and Pearl's reaction to it are a source of continual pain. On the surface Hester is uncomplaining and somber, but her passions have been redirected into thoughts about the individual's role in society.

2. Hester's free speculation about life and her abandonment of Puritan values, if known, would have been held a far deadlier crime than adultery.

3. Hester sees little hope for improvement in her condition and, at times, considers killing both Pearl and herself and taking her chances in the afterlife.

4. Hester believes that the whole of society must be torn down and the rules of conduct as proscribed by the Puritan leaders must be done away with. Secondly, men must change their attitudes towards women and their capabilities. Finally, women must change their images of themselves and take the means of power equally with men.

5. "Office" means the job for which it was intended. The letter was intended to make Hester remorseful of her sin and eager to keep in line with Puritan values. In fact, it has done the opposite, even bringing her to the point of considering murder and suicide.

6. Hester feels her promise not to reveal Chillingworth's identity is allowing the doctor to torment the minister, causing his physical deterioration.

7. Chillingworth feels he has kept the minister from being imprisoned or even executed by keeping his part in the adultery secret. In fact, it has been the doctor's continued care that has kept Dimmesdale alive.

8. The doctor, now aware of the fiendish person he has become

in his pursuit of revenge, feels Dimmesdale has done this to him and is therefore even more deserving of punishment. He takes no responsibility for his actions.

9. Although Hester has not been open with Pearl about the letter, this is the first time she has ever lied to Pearl. Pearl knows Hester is lying. She cannot bring herself to tell the child about her illegitimacy and says she wears the letter only for its value as a decoration.

10. Pearl is beginning to show traits of affection for her mother, and Hester considers confiding in her. Another change is refelected in Hester's stern warning to Pearl to be quiet as she continues asking about the letter. Before this time she could not find it within herself to be harsh with the child.

Sample Essay Topics

1. Discuss the Puritan moral law and the crime of independent thinking.

2. Compare Puritan parenting and Hester's raising of Pearl.

3. How do Hester, Dimmesdale, and Chillingworth differ in their acceptance of what seems to be their fate?

SECTION SEVEN

Hester Attempts to Take Charge

(Chapters 16–19)

Chapter 16: "A Forest Walk"

Summary

After several days of attempting to meet with and tell Dimmesdale the truth about her former husband, Hester learns that he will be returning from a visit to another minister along a path through the forest. She wishes to speak with him in the openness of nature, but she is also aware of the parallel between the actual wilderness and the moral wilderness in which she feels she has been wandering.

Pearl has been playing in the patches of the sunshine that shifting clouds have caused. She teases her mother that the sunshine is avoiding her. Pearl does catch the light, but when Hester approaches and attempts to grasp it, the sunlight disappears.

Pearl asks for a story about the Black Man and repeats a story she had overheard at a house Hester had visited the evening before. In this story, among the people who have visited the Black Man in the Forest at night is Hester, who wears his mark, the scarlet letter. Hester agrees with the story; she has met with the Black

Man and does wear his mark. As they talk, they approach a brook, and Pearl remarks that it sounds very sad. Hearing footsteps and anticipating Dimmesdale, Hester attempts to send Pearl off to play. The child remarks that the minister's hand over his heart may point to the spot where the Black Man put his mark upon the minister, then skips off to play. Hester watches the minister, listless and haggard, approach the spot where the path crosses the brook.

Analysis

Hawthorne uses the forest as a symbol in several ways. It is the abode of the Black Man, a wilderness where the devil and the heathen Indians roam. Those who venture out into the forest at night are most assuredly meeting with the devil. Hester admits to meeting symbolically with the devil and at one point feels she is wandering in a moral wilderness. A second reference to the forest is as a place where, in contrast to the strictness of the Puritan settlement, people and events here are open and natural. Later, Hawthorne will present the forest as a place of potential.

An ongoing motif is Hawthorne's symbolic use of light and dark in the novel. Here the sunlight favors Pearl while the sunshine, like happiness, eludes Hester.

Chapter 17:
"The Pastor and His Parishioner"

Summary

The meeting of Hester Prynne and Arthur Dimmesdale is awkward at first. After speaking of unimportant matters, both confess that they have not found peace. The minister tells of his continued hypocrisy and wishes for one person before whom he could daily be known for the sinner he is. Hester replies that there is such a person and he "dwellest with him under the same roof." Dimmesdale is furious with Hester for concealing Chillingworth's identity, and allowing him to go through the horror of living with Chillingworth. Hester sees the depth of evil she has permitted and tries to explain why she allowed the deception. However, she concludes that " . . . a lie is never good, even though death threatens on the other side."

Dimmesdale condemns and rejects her, yet she pleads to him for forgiveness, telling him that Chillingworth is her husband.

It is Chillingworth who has committed the vilest sin, according to Dimmesdale. He has sought continual revenge in a calculated manner; the two lovers, while sinners, did not set out to hurt anyone.

Dimmesdale wonders what course Chillingworth's revenge will now take and asks Hester for help. "The judgment of God is on me. . . It is too mighty for me to struggle with!" She demands that he be strong and formulates a plan. The minister can leave the Puritan settlement and restart his life in the wilderness or in Europe. When he replies that he has not the strength to begin anew, Hester says he will not be going alone, that she has strength enough for both of them.

Analysis

The dark wood in which Hester and Dimmesdale meet and their separation of seven years makes them doubt the reality of the moment. The dramatic interchanges in which forgiveness is asked, withheld, and given and in which plans are made reveal much about the two characters and their futures. Hester is strong and is able to both analyze the situation and plan for the future. She demands that Dimmesdale be strong and take control over his life. He doubts whether he can do anything about his life until Hester tells him that he will not have to leave alone.

In this chapter the forest is offered as a place of escape. Though mastering the wilderness seems beyond the minister's physical and emotional strength, he comes to realize that outside the settlement are places where a person may start a new life.

Chapter 18: "A Flood of Sunshine"

Summary

The narrator explains the source of Hester's boldness. Ostracized by the community, she has learned to think for herself, free of the strict boundaries proscribed by the Puritans. In contrast, Arthur Dimmesdale is a representative of that system, a priest, and therefore bound all the more by it. When Dimmesdale agrees to leave with Hester, they both feel a resurgence of hope. Hester symbolically tears off the scarlet letter and tosses it into the bushes. Rather than landing in the brook which could carry it away, the scrap of cloth lands among the fallen leaves on the edge of the water.

Hester lets down her hair, and as she does so, sunlight bathes the scene. She wants father and daughter to know each other and so calls to Pearl who is standing in another patch of sunlight. During this interval she has been playing with the plants and animals about her. The narrator suggests that one version of the tale implies that a savage wolf had come to Pearl to be petted. Because she sees the minister still with her mother, Pearl comes back slowly.

Analysis

This chapter contrasts the two characters as they plan their future actions. The great forces opposing the minister's leaving are noted; and though he agrees to go along with Hester's plan, we can see that it will be extremely difficult for him to do so.

As they feel an initial release from their burdens, the sunlight which bathes them is not, the narrator tells us, a symbolic blessing from Providence, but Nature's sympathetic reaction to the joining of the hearts of two lovers. Pearl is standing in a separate patch of sunlight, one which comes down upon her " . . . through an arch of boughs," suggesting a religious significance to her light in contrast to theirs. Careful reading will permit a reader to determine when Hawthorne is suggesting the light is of a divine, demonic, magical, or natural origin.

The narrator also calls our attention to the fact that the scarlet letter, tossed aside by Hester, falls short of being carried away by the little brook, a suggestion that Hester will not be rid of the stigma so easily.

The narrator also offers differing versions of Pearl at play. The dramatic realism of the meeting he has just related is offset by the fanciful image of a wolf allowing Pearl to pet him, reminding us that the novel is a retelling of a supposed historical event intended to be read at multiple levels.

Pearl's reluctance to hurry back to the reunited lovers suggests that she might be a cause of trouble to the plans Hester and the minister have made.

Chapter 19: "The Child at Brookside"

Summary

As Hester and Dimmesdale await Pearl's return, the minister confesses his ongoing dread of the child, the living testimony of his sin, while Hester remarks on her beauty and her fitful moods. Pearl responds to her mother's call but remains in a patch of sunlight on the opposite side of the brook, refusing to come closer. When Dimmesdale reaches his hand up to his heart, Pearl points to the spot on her mother's breast where the scarlet letter should be. In response to Hester's promptings to join them, Pearl goes into a wild tantrum, pointing to Hester's bodice. To pacify her, Hester points to the scarlet letter lying by the side of the stream and asks Pearl to bring it to her. Pearl insists that her mother pick it up. Thinking she will soon be rid of the stigma permanently, Hester does so, but placing it once more in its accustomed place makes her feel a sense of inevitable doom. Pearl spontaneously kisses her mother, then the scarlet letter itself, an act which pains Hester greatly.

When Pearl asks about the minister, standing a distance from them, Hester replies that he loves them and wants to meet her. Pearl wants to know if the love is great enough to have the minister walk back, hand in hand, with them to the village. Hester has to drag an uncooperative Pearl back to the minister. Pearl washes off his unwelcomed kiss and remains apart while the two complete the details of their escape.

Analysis

The foreshadowing noted at the end of Chapter 18 is fulfilled as Pearl refuses to accept her mother without the familiar scarlet letter. She insists her mother take up the symbol herself and refuses to accept the minister's kiss. Here, in an allegorical sense, Pearl is their living conscience, reminding the two of their situation, their responsibilities, and the impossibility of escaping their guilt.

Dimmesdale's aversion to the child has several explanations. He does not have a natural affinity for children, and Pearl's personality marks her as a difficult child. Her very existence is a constant reminder to him of his sin, while her features hold possible clues to his identity as her father.

Pearl's refusal to join Hester and Dimmesdale can be interpreted on multiple levels. She is a young child who has been excluded from their talk. As a child she is upset with any changes in her mother, and the removal of the scarlet letter is frightening to her. If she is the symbolic embodiment of the scarlet letter, neither she nor it can be tossed away. On the allegorical level, Pearl functions here as an agent of the divine, preventing Hester from avoiding the consequences of her actions.

Study Questions

1. Why does Hester prefer to meet with Dimmesdale in the forest rather than in the settlement?

2. What significance can be attributed to the play of sunlight on Pearl and Hester?

3. What story does Pearl hear of her mother's involvement with the Black Man of the Forest?

4. What are Dimmesdale's reactions when Hester tells him Chillingworth's true identity?

5. What effect does Hester have upon Dimmesdale?

6. How does Pearl fit into the forest setting?

7. Why does Pearl refuse to retrieve the scarlet letter herself?

8. Why does Pearl insist that the scarlet letter be replaced?

9. What is the effect on Hester when she replaces the letter on her bosom?

10. What is the significance of Pearl's reaction to the minister?

Answers

1. Hester prefers the openness of the forest for their important talk. She also fears the interference of Chillingworth if the two meet anywhere in the settlement.

2. Here, sunlight seems to symbolize happiness and acceptance of the individual by nature. Pearl delights in the light while it eludes Hester when she reaches for it.

3. Pearl has overheard rumors that her mother meets regularly with the devil in the forest. Hester denies this and admits to meeting with the devil once and receiving the scarlet letter from him. Hester is referring here to her instance of adultery but an argument can be made that her independent thinking is her ongoing sin, thus representing her ongoing meetings with the devil.

4. Dimmesdale is astonished to learn that Chillingworth is Hester's former husband. He gives her an evil look and refuses at first to forgive her. Hester holds him fiercely and insists that he forgive her.

5. Unable to think or act clearly, Dimmesdale says, "Be thou strong for me!" It is Hester who excites him with the possibilitiy of escape.

6. Pearl moves naturally and happily in the forest. The sunlight delights her, the berries feed her, the flowers adorn her, and the forest animals accept her as a natural part of the scene.

7. Pearl wants her mother to retrieve the scarlet letter herself and put it back on.

8. The narrator suggests that Pearl may be reluctant to return from the natural world and directly states that she feels excluded from her mother's affection by the presence of Dimmesdale. Dimmesdale says that Pearl could be having a natu-

ral reaction to seeing a change in her mother's appearance or could very well be a devilish spirit.

9. Hester, forced to put the letter back on, has a sense of "inevitable doom." She puts up her hair back under her cap and again becomes the somber person she had been for seven years.

10. Pearl focuses on the need for Dimmesdale to openly acknowledge his lover and illegitimate daughter. Pearl's washing off of his kiss sets us up for her eventual acceptance of his kiss in the climatic scene of the novel.

Suggested Essay Topics

1. Compare and contrast the personalities of Hester and Dimmesdale in the forest. How does Hawthorne use the forest as a multiple symbol?

2. Discuss the use of sunlight and shade in these chapters.

Dimmesdale Reconsiders

(Chapters 20–22)

Chapter 20: "The Minister in a Maze"

Summary

As he leaves Hester and Pearl behind on the forest path, Dimmesdale reviews the plan he and Hester have devised for escape. Hester is to secure passage for the three of them on a ship now in port and bound for England. When Hester tells him that it will probably be four days until their departure, the minister is glad. Three days from now he will preach the Election Day sermon and has decided that it is the ideal time to confess his guilt and end his career as a preacher.

The dramatic changes in his life now rejuvenate the minister, and he experiences strange transformations and impulses. He wants to tell people about the new Dimmesdale, to whisper sacrilegious ideas to a church official and an old lady, and to give impure suggestions to a young maiden obviously enamored of him. These temptations lead the minister to conclude that the plan devised in the forest was, in fact, a pact with the devil, who even now is taking over his soul. Mistress Hibbins appears at this time.

By congratulating him on his meeting with the devil in the forest, she confirms his suspicions.

Dimmesdale returns to his study and resumes work on the Election Day sermon. He refuses Chillingworth's offer of medicines to see him through the election day and returns to his task with energy. He is still writing as the morning light finds him.

Analysis

Agreeing to Hester's plan has dissolved the stalemate of public hypocrisy and private suffering that Dimmesdale has lived with for seven years, and his mind is now freed to consider possibilities. He feels a new power in his step and in his ability to influence people around him by creating scandal in their minds. These great temptations and a conversation with a reputed witch cause him to return to more familiar thoughts, that he should not do the work of the devil and that he is a powerless pawn with a destiny to be played out on the present stage. Being drawn in one direction by Hester has caused him to pull back and to act with a greater determination as he feels fate is directing him to.

Chapter 21: "The New England Holiday"

Summary

The settlement is crowded with visitors and townspeople interested in seeing the new governor take office. Hester, with Pearl by her side, views the scene with mixed emotions. She is looking, for what might be the last time, at the society which has been her life and her torture for seven long years. She is anticipating the freedom which will be hers in a few hours. Pearl, dressed in a bright dress, reflects in her actions the mixed emotions which her mother is hiding beneath a calm exterior. She demands an explanation for the gathering and is told all are here for the holiday procession of soldiers and officials. To questions about the minister, Hester replies that they must not greet him publicly today.

The narrator describes the scenes and events of this holiday and the attitudes behind them. Many remember the wilder celebrations of England, and, while there are no skits or singing or

dancing, the Puritans have lightened up their usual somber lifestyle with a procession and with some sporting competitions: in this case, wrestling and fighting with quarterstaffs. A swordfight is broken up by the town beadle, much to the disappointment of the crowd. In addition to Indians, rough-looking sailors can be seen, drinking and smoking in contradiction to the stern Puritan laws. Roger Chillingworth is seen talking earnestly with a ship's captain, who later recognizes Hester among the crowd and approaches her. The captain tells Hester that making ready one more berth for her party will be no problem. Chillingworth is going with them. Hester then glimpses the old doctor smiling at her from across the market-place and realizes her plan to leave is coming undone.

Analysis

The narrator here attempts to give the reader an understanding of the varied attitudes among the Puritans. Normally somber, they did brighten up for state occasions, intertwined as these were with religious office. A few of the quieter English customs, processions and sporting events were transplanted to this early colony. The Puritans interacted with those about them—Indians, traders, and sailors—tolerating their differences. The narrator comments sardonically that they have lightened up to a point equal to that of people who are greatly troubled.

Hester's helping the poor and the troubled has acquainted her with the sea captain, and so there is no scandal in her talking with him. News that Chillingworth is going to be on the same ship is the beginning of the unraveling of her plan to escape.

Chapter 22: "The Procession"

Summary

March music is heard, and even Pearl is momentarily transfixed by the sight and sound of the musicians, the military men, the civil authorities, and lastly, the Reverend Mr. Dimmesdale as he is escorted to the meeting-house. He walks with unusual energy, and as Hester looks upon him, she senses that he is beyond her reach. In contrast to the closeness they shared in the forest, he seems a player in a drama and she, a mere spectator. Even Pearl is unsure that she recognizes the man.

Mistress Hibbins begins a conversation with Hester about the transformation in the minister. Over Hester's protests, the woman goes on to speak of the minister's dark secrets and his possible revelation of them in the open air. Dimmesdale's sermon begins, and Hester, unable to get into the meeting-house, takes a spot in the crowd near the scaffold.

The powerful sounds of Dimmesdale's voice delivering his sermon can be heard outside in the market-place. While Hester and others listen, not quite able to make out the words, Pearl runs about, first investigating an Indian, then, a group of sailors. One, the ship captain, gives her a gold chain and asks her to carry a message to her mother: the doctor will bring the gentleman aboard, and she need worry only about herself and her child.

While she is digesting this painful news, Hester and her scarlet letter become the center of the attention among strangers who have heard of, but not seen, the red symbol. Their attention soon attracts others, and Hester finds herself at the center of a ring of strangers, seamen, Indians, and townspeople.

Analysis

The procession allows the narrator to compare and contrast the groups that parade by with both their counterparts in Europe at that time and with those of Hawthorne's age, the 1850s. The military men in armor and plumes carried themselves with a haughtiness that showed they considered the call to arms a high calling. The magistrates who followed showed a dignity and seriousness of purpose, rather than any other talent, that suited them for governing the colony. Last and most important was the religious leader, one whose profession enjoyed " . . . the almost worshipful respect of the community."

Any lingering hope that the lovers can rise above their problems is dashed by the distant look about Dimmesdale as he proceeds to the meeting-house. Hester recognizes the great gulf between them, and even Pearl is not sure that this is the same man she met in the forest. The conversation with the reputed witch who speaks of the forest meeting of Hester and the minister shows more public unraveling of their secrets.

Hester endures many painful barbs in this chapter: Dimmesdale's aloofness as he passes, Mistress Hibbins' prying questions and her prophecies, the captain's message about Chillingworth's intentions, and the hurtful stares of the people as she stands by the scaffold. This last scene, where people begin staring at Hester's letter for little reason, allows us to see that Hester has not progressed very far in seven years. Only the face of the sympathetic young mother, now dead, is missing from the opening scene of the novel, when the Puritan women stared and commented on Hester's disgrace. Unaware that the same stigma marked both Hester and Dimmesdale, an observer might have noted an ironic contrast between the minister, surrounded by attentive and adorous listeners in the meeting-house, and the adulterous woman, surrounded by a more hostile crowd in the market-place.

Study Questions

1. What is Hester's plan for Dimmesdale, Pearl, and herself?

2. What is Dimmesdale tempted to do as he returns to his room? Why?

3. What decision does he make as he reaches his lodging?

4. What does the Puritan celebration tell about their values?

5. How has Chillingworth interfered with Hester's plan?

6. What does the procession show about Puritan values?

7. What is the minister's mental state as he walks to the meeting-house? What effect does he have upon Hester?

8. Where is Hester standing during Dimmesdale's sermon?

9. Why does Hester become the center of the crowd's attention? What irony does the narrator see in the scene?

10. What is Pearl doing during the sermon?

Answers

1. Hester will arrange passage to England for the three of them with a ship's captain who is leaving in four days.

2. As the minister encounters people on his way he is tempted to suggest obscene religious practices to a deacon, heretical comments about doctrines to a pious woman, and impure ideas to a young maiden. His weakened mind is not accustomed to thinking outside the basic Puritan guidelines.

3. Since he is scheduled to deliver an important sermon one day before the escape to England, Dimmesdale is moved to write a new and more powerful sermon. The encounter with Hibbins causes him to pull back from the wild thoughts he

has been experiencing and to reconsider Hester's plan for them.

4. The Puritans take the transfer of political power very seriously, intertwined as it is with religious power. Remnants of English attitudes remain with them, but celebration are restricted to only modest changes from their somber routines. The narrator comments that even as they celebrated, the Puritans looked like people undergoing great troubles.

5. Somehow Chillingworth has found out about the plan and has booked passage to England on the same ship.

6. The solemnity accorded the procession is the same the Puritans gave to most activities. The order in which the groups marched showed their relative importance to the community: the military first, the civil authorities next, and the religious, last and most important.

7. The minister is walking with new-found energy, seemingly oblivious to the crowd and the moment. Hester is dismayed at the remoteness of his look and fears her plan has little hope of being fulfilled.

8. By coincidence, Hester, unable to get into the packed meeting-house, stands next to the scaffold.

9. Newcomers to the village had heard of but had not seen the woman with the scarlet letter. Now aware of her, they cause others to stare at Hester. While she and her letter are the center of one crowd, Dimmesdale, with the burden on his chest, ironically is the center of another group.

10. Pearl, in typical fashion, is skipping about, investigating Indians and sailors. One, the sea captain, gives her a gold chain and a message about Chillingworth for her mother.

Suggested Essay Topics

1. Discuss Puritan values as exemplified by their celebrations.

2. Explain Dimmesdale's emotional state since leaving Hester.

3. Discuss Hawthorne's use of irony and coincidence in these chapters.

4. Discuss whether Mistress Hibbins is real or allegorical.

Resolution

(Chapters 23–24)

Chapter 23:
"The Revelation of The Scarlet Letter"

Summary

Dimmesdale has finished his sermon, and as people exit the meeting-house, they proclaim the wisdom in his inspired words. He has spoken of the special relationship between God and the New England communities and prophesied a great future for the people. Now the march music begins anew, and all are to proceed to the town-hall for a solemn banquet.

Even as he is honored as being at the high point of his career, Dimmesdale looks exhausted, and people fear he will fall at any moment. He rejects the offered arm of Reverend Wilson and continues on until he encounters Hester and Pearl standing by the scaffold. Governor Bellingham steps forward to offer assistance but is stopped by a look from the minister. The rest of the procession continues on, but Dimmesdale calls to Hester and Pearl.

As Pearl clasps his knees and Hester comes towards him " . . . as if impelled by inevitable fate," Chillingworth protests and catches him by the arm. Dimmesdale waves him off and again calls to Hester, who helps him up the steps to the scaffold. Chillingworth

follows. "Hadst thou sought the whole earth over," said he, looking darkly at the clergyman, "there was no one place so secret—no high place or lowly place, where thou couldst have escaped me—save on this very scaffold!"

The noonday sun shines down upon the Reverend Dimmesdale as he announces to the entire community that one sinner in their midst has remained hidden for seven long years. With that, he tears open his robe to reveal something on his breast. He sinks to the scaffold and is supported by Hester, his head against her bosom. He forgives Chillingworth and asks Pearl for a kiss. The girl responds with a kiss and tears, and we are told that a spell has been broken. In the future Pearl will become a secure young woman, no longer a source of anguish to her mother.

Hester asks whether they shall meet again. The minister, in his dying words, tells her that the law they broke makes it a vain hope that they should have an everlasting and perfect union. Dimmesdale does thank God for his mercy—for the burning torture upon his breast, the presence of Chillingworth to give him further pain, and the opportunity ". . . to die this death of triumphant ignominy before the people," all of which have helped to save his soul.

Analysis

The change in Reverend Dimmesdale after delivering his triumphal sermon is dramatic. He totters forward as a man with hardly any life in him. If his great objective was to confess upon the scaffold, it would seem he would be highly energized as he approached the spot, yet it is only after seeing Hester and Pearl standing near the scaffold that the minister pauses. While it is likely that Dimmesdale fully intended to confess his hidden sin at this point, Hawthorne's wording does not make this very clear. That Dimmesdale rejects assistance from Wilson, a representative of the church and from Bellingham, a representative of the state, can be taken as symbolic of his determination to do what he has to do on his own.

This, the final of three scaffold scenes in the novel, brings all four major characters to the place of punishment and atonement. Pearl, whose very existence is the result of a broken Commandment, is able to kiss her father and, no longer needed as the allegorical tormentor of Hester, become a normal person. Hester, publicly punished for seven years and yet not inwardly remorseful, returns to the place of her initial humiliation. Dimmesdale, adulterer and hypocrite, finally stands, in the light of day, where he should have shared the public scorn seven years ago. Chillingworth, whose sin has been called the blackest of the several presented by the story, is revealed to the community as a vengeful creature who by intention set out to torment another human being.

Of the four major players, Dimmesdale seems to be the central focus. Pearl's only sin is being born, and she is allowed to find happiness. Hester, though she remains a strong character who wins our sympathy for her ability to endure, has few options in her conflict with Puritan morality. She is an example of the women made relatively powerless by the way societies have been set up, an idea expanded upon by Hawthorne in Chapter 13. Chillingworth, though the most detestable of the characters, was initially a kindly man who is caught up in an obsession much as Hester and Dimmesdale were in their act of adultery. They were overcome by a need for love while Chillingworth is overcome by a need for revenge. Dimmesdale, though, has several additional conflicts—with himself, that he cannot be truthful; with his followers, who see him not as a hypocrite, but as a holy man; and with his God, who requires atonement for the transgression Dimmesdale is guilty of. It is his inability to resolve these conflicts that compound the pain and sins of the others.

Chapter 24: "The Conclusion"

Summary
In the days that follow Dimmesdale's death many opinions are offered for the letter "A" that was seen on the minister's chest. Some say he inflicted it upon himself, others say that Chillingworth caused it to appear through the use of drugs and magic, and still others speculate that personal remorse and divine judgment combined to put it upon the minister's chest. Again, by presenting multiple versions of an incident, the storyteller allows the reader's mind to choose the most likely version and thus to think more deeply about the idea he is presenting.

Others deny that any such mark even existed. They maintain that the minister was not guilty of any misdeed, and that he simply used his final moments to make yet another impression on his congregation. The narrator disregards this last version and tells us that the most important moral to be learned from Dimmesdale's experience is "Be true! Be true! Be true! Show freely to the world, if not your worst, yet some trait whereby the worst may be inferred!"

Chillingworth, with his life's purpose gone, withers away and dies within a year. The narrator speculates that hate and love may be much the same thing, and that in the spiritual world Chillingworth and Dimmesdale, two who were victims of each other,

may find their hatred turned to love. The doctor leaves much property, both in the colonies and in England, to Pearl, who leaves Salem with her mother soon after Chillingworth's death.

Years later reports say that Hester Prynne returned to Salem
and her cottage and resumed wearing the scarlet letter. While in-
dications are that Pearl has married into royalty in England, Hester
has returned. "Here had been her sin: here, her sorrow; and here,

her penitence." Hester has become a counselor of troubled people, especially women, and assures them that at some brighter time in the future relations between men and women will be on " . . . a surer ground of mutual happiness." At her death Hester is buried near the grave of Dimmesdale with one tombstone, bearing a coat of arms carved with a single letter "A," serving for both.

Analysis

This chapter serves three major functions. It speculates on morals to be derived from the story, attempts to produce a happy ending for at least one of the characters, and ties up loose ends in a fitting sort of way. Hester's identity is so interwoven with the place of her sin and with the scarlet letter that she returns to both, even-

tually to be buried near, but not with, her lover, fulfilling the minister's declaration that theirs would always be an imperfect union. Chillingworth, driven by revenge, an obsession similar to the lovers' passion, is consumed by his sin as they were by theirs, but partially redeems himself with his legacy to Pearl. Her escape to a happy life away from Salem is the best that Hawthorne could do to satisfy his readers' need for a balance of happiness and sadness.

Among the sins, hypocrisy is put forth as the one most controllable and the one causing the most damage to all, for it compounds the effects of other sins. Admitting his guilt with Hester would have precluded the seven years of personal torment for Hester and Dimmesdale and prevented himself from being consumed with vengeance. If the narrator says "Be True!" is the moral to be most directly drawn from the life of Reverend Dimmesdale, it might equally be said of the other two sinners. Chillingworth's taking on a false identity and Hester's concealment of this fact from Dimmesdale would seem to make them equally worthy of blame.

The chapter's last scene, that of two graves sharing a simple headstone, dramatically focuses our attention on the symbol which in all of its manifestations remains central to the novel.

Study Questions

1. What is the topic and mood of Dimmesdale's sermon?

2. Describe the minister's condition after the speech, and tell which people offer him assistance.

3. Where are the four major characters during the final scaffold scene?

4. What changes occur in Pearl? What does she accept from Dimmesdale?

5. What moral does the narrator say is central to the story?

6. What are the various versions of what was seen on Dimmesdale's chest?

7. What is the effect of Dimmesdale's confession on Chillingworth?

8. What is the effect of Chillingworth's legacy to Pearl?

9. Describe the circumstances of Hester's return to Salem.

10. Are the two lovers ever united?

Answers

1. Dimmesdale's sermon is a passionate and surprisingly positive one about the relationship of God to the Puritan community and about the "high and glorious destiny for the newly gathered people of the Lord."

2. Dimmesdale seems near death. He rejects the assistance of Reverend Wilson and of Governor Bellingham, but accepts the help of Hester as he mounts the scaffold.

3. All four, Hester, Pearl, Dimmesdale, and Chillingworth, are now on the scaffold.

4. Dimmesdale's kiss acknowledges Pearl as his child, and breaks the spell which seems to have held Pearl captive. She cries and, we are told, will be a normal person from this moment onward.

5. "Be true! Be true! Be true!" The inability of Dimmesdale to be honest is pointed to as the central cause of the ongoing distress.

6. The narrator again is ambiguous. A red letter "A" was seen and was said to be either cut or burnt in by Dimmesdale, made to appear by his guilt feelings and heaven's judgment, put there by Chillingworth's medicines or magic, or was never there at all.

7. Frustrated by Dimmesdale's confession and death, Chillingworth withers away and dies within a year.

8. The great amount of land left to Pearl allows her and Hester to leave Boston.

9. Several years later Hester returns to Boston. She takes up her residence in the cottage and resumes her drab dress accented by the scarlet letter.

10. Dimmesdale's last words presumed that their sin meant they would never have a perfect union. In death they are buried near, but not beside, each other. Whether Hester and Dimmesdale are united in heaven is left unsaid.

Suggested Essay Topics

1. How does Pearl change after the scaffold scene?

2. Discuss Hester's role as a counselor of troubled women.

3. Discuss Hester and Dimmesdale as pawns of fate.

4. How is the phrase "Be true" a central theme of the story?

5. How are Hester, Dimmesdale, Pearl, and Chillingworth redeemed by the end of the novel?

Sample Analytical Paper Topics

The following paper topics are designed to test your understanding of the novel as a whole and to analyze important themes and literary devices. Following each question is a sample outline to help get you started.

Topic #1

Discuss Hawthorne's blend of realism, symbolism, and allegory in *The Scarlet Letter.*

Outline

I.   Thesis Statement: The Scarlet Letter *is a blend of realism, symbolism, and allegory.*

II. Realism in *The Scarlet Letter*

    A. Historical setting

    B. Psychological exploration of characters

    C. Realistic dialogue

III. Symbolism in *The Scarlet Letter*

    A. The letter and its obvious manifestations

    B. Pearl as a human manifestation of the letter

    C. The settings as symbols

        1. The settlement

      2.   The forest

      3.   The scaffold

      4.   The market-place

IV. Allegory in *The Scarlet Letter*

   A. Definition

   B. Character types

      1.   The beadle

      2.   Hester

      3.   Dimmesdale

      4.   Chillingworth

      5.   Pearl

Topic #2

How are Puritans represented in *The Scarlet Letter?*

Outline

I.   Thesis Statement: *Hawthorne's opinion of the Puritans may be understood by examining their actions within the novel and the narrator's comment on them.*

II. Historical background on the Puritans

III. Hawthorne's ancestors as described in "The Custom-House" essay

IV. The Puritan's actions in *The Scarlet Letter*

   A. The ministers

   B. The common people

      1.   Attitudes toward work and relaxation

      2.   Attitudes toward their religious beliefs

      3.   Attitudes toward Hester and Pearl

V.   The narrator's comments about Puritans

   A. Negative comments

B. Positive comments

Topic #3

Discuss Hester Prynne's conflicts with herself, with others, and with Nature.

Outline

I. Thesis Statement: *Hester Prynne has several conflicts, and as these are resolved, her character is revealed.*

II. Types of conflict possible

     A. Conflict with self

     B. Conflict with another

     C. Conflict with a group

     D. Conflict with Nature

     E. Conflict with the supernatural

III. Hester in conflict with herself

     A. Accepts her actions as wrong

     B. Retains a sense of pride

IV. Hester in conflict with another

     A. Settles initial conflict with Chillingworth

     B. Challenges Chillingworth about her promise

     C. Attempts to outmaneuver Chillingworth

V. Hester in conflict with a group

     A. Accepts the society's punishment with patience

     B. Fights the power structure and Dimmesdale to keep Pearl

     C. Her thoughts defy conventional teaching

     D. Resumes her punishment years later of her own choosing

VI. Hester in conflict with nature

     A. Resists the "Black Man of the Forest"

    B.   Accepts the natural forest as promising freedom

VII. Hester in conflict with the supernatural

    A.   Resists the "Black Man of the Forest"

    B.   Allows God to judge her sin without any pleading for mercy

SECTION ELEVEN

Bibliography

Baym, Nina. *The Scarlet Letter: A Reading*. Boston: Twayn, 1986.

Gerber, John C. *Twentieth Century Interpretations of The Scarlet Letter*. Englewood Cliffs, New Jersey: Prentice Hall, 1968.

Hawthorne, Nathaniel. *The Scarlet Letter*. Norwalk, Connecticut: Heritage Press, 1973.

The Scarlet Letter; an annotatated text, backgrounds, and sources. New York: Norton, 1962.

Introducing...

MAXnotes

REA's Literature Study Guide

MAXnotes™ offer a fresh look at masterpieces of literature, presented in a li
and interesting fashion. **MAXnotes**™ offer the essentials of what you should kr
about the work, including outlines, explanations and discussions of the p
character lists, analyses, and historical context. **MAXnotes**™ are designed to h
you think independently about literary works by raising various issues and thou
provoking ideas and questions. Written by literary experts who currently teach
subject, **MAXnotes**™ enhance your understanding and enjoyment of the work

---

Available **MAXnotes**™ include the following:

Animal Farm	**Huckleberry Finn**	**Of Mice and Men**
Beowulf	**I Know Why the**	**The Odyssey**
The Canterbury Tales	**Caged Bird Sings**	**Paradise Lost**
Death of a Salesman	**The Iliad**	**Plato's Republic**
Divine Comedy I-Inferno	**Julius Caesar**	**A Raisin in the Sun**
Gone with the Wind	**King Lear**	**Romeo and Juliet**
The Grapes of Wrath	**Les Misérables**	**The Scarlet Letter**
Great Expectations	**Macbeth**	**A Tale of Two Cities**
The Great Gatsby	**Moby Dick**	**To Kill a Mockingbird**
Hamlet	**1984**	

RESEARCH & EDUCATION ASSOCIATION
61 Ethel Road W. • Piscataway, New Jersey 08854
Phone: (908) 819-8880

Please send me more information about MAXnotes™.

Name _____

Address _____

City _____ State _____ Zip _____

he High School Tutors

HIGH SCHOOL TUTORS series is based on the same principle as the more prehensive **PROBLEM SOLVERS**, but is specifically designed to meet the needs of school students. REA has recently revised all the books in this series to include expanded ew sections, new material, and newly-designed covers. This makes the books even more ctive in helping students to cope with these difficult high school subjects.

If you would like more information about any of these books,
complete the coupon below and return it to us or go to your local bookstore.

RESEARCH & EDUCATION ASSOCIATION
51 Ethel Road W. • Piscataway, New Jersey 08854
Phone: (908) 819-8880

Please send me more information about your High School Tutor books.

ame _____

ddress _____

ity _____ State _____ Zip _____